DISCARDED

ESPIONAGE & DISINFORMATION

CLIVE GIFFORD

Heinemann Library
Chicago, Illinois

Photo research, design and illustration by Trocadero Publishing, An Electra Media Group Enterprise, Suite 204, 74 Pitt Street, Sydney, Australia
Printed and bound in Hong Kong and China by Wing King Tong

10 09 08 07 06
10 9 8 7 6 5 4 3 2 1

Library of Congress Cataloging-in-Publication Data

Gifford, Clive.
  Espionage & disinformation : the unseen world / Clive Gifford.
    p. cm. -- (Influence and persuasion)
  Includes bibliographical references and index.
  ISBN 1-4034-7652-7 (lib. bdg.)
  1. Espionage. I. Title: Espionage and disinformation. II. Title. III. Series.
  JF1525.I6G54 2006
  327.12--dc22
                          2005015148
Acknowledgments
Brand X Pictures 24, 25, 33, 47; Comstock Images 19, 26 (bottom), 48; Corbis/Bob Battersby (Eye Ubiquitous) 11; Department of Defence Australia 58; Digital Stock 16; Electra Collection 26 (top), 36, 37; Flat Earth Picture Gallery 5, 18, 50, 51; International Spy Museum 13, 28, 42, 44, 52, 54; Kobal Collection/Orion Pictures 20; Kobal Collection/ United Artists 38; Kobal Collection/Universal Pictures 40; Newspix 21; Oronsay Imagery/ Scott Brodie 15, 22, 41, 49; Popperfoto 32, 34, 35 (top), 35 (bottom); Reuters/Ian Hodgson 57; Rex Features 29; United Nations 31; US Air Force 45, 46; US Army 6, 7 (bottom), 53; US Department of Defense 14, 17; US Department of Homeland Security 12, 55; US National Archives 7 (top), 8, 9, 27, 30, 39

Cover photograph reproduced with permission of Getty Images/Taxi

Contents

Introduction

Every country, company, and military force has information they strive to keep secret. This information is highly prized by others and can be the difference between success or failure in business, between victory or defeat in battle, and whether a government or ruler stays in power or is toppled. This information is known as intelligence, and comes in many different forms. It can be military details about troops, their location, and planned movements. It can be political secrets about what alliances one nation intends to form with others. It can also be technical secrets such as details of scientific research or the workings of a new weapon.

Espionage is the practice of obtaining secrets from rivals or enemies in order to gain some sort of edge or advantage over them. It is most frequently performed by government intelligence organizations, which exist in almost all countries. Espionage is also commonly known as spying and is illegal. But this does not stop nations from spying in secret on both hostile and friendly countries. Espionage can be the only way to obtain important information about rival countries, their future intentions, and their military and economic capabilities.

Disinformation is false or misleading information announced publicly or leaked by a government or intelligence organization. It is produced with the goal of deliberately deceiving the people who receive the information. Although the practice of feeding untrue information to enemy armies has been used for centuries, the term disinformation is a 20th-century invention. It comes from the Russian, *dezinformatsia*, a term coined by the Soviet Union's KGB intelligence agency.

Standing guard at the most heavily fortified frontier in the world, at Panmunjom, Korea.

Espionage's Role & Influence

Espionage work is mostly carried out in secret but it can influence the policies and actions that countries decide to take. Intelligence can persuade governments to take a particular course of action. For example, intelligence from a range of sources, including human agents, spy satellites, and planes, convinced the United States and British governments that Iraq had chemical and biological weapons known as weapons of mass destruction (WMD). Intelligence is not always reliable but it is often influential. The intelligence about Iraq and its WMD capability helped the U.S. and UK leaders decide to invade Iraq in 2003.

A U.S. Army Abrams tank patrols the streets of Baghdad in the early stages of the Iraq conflict. Espionage played a key role in the decision to send forces into Iraq to depose the Saddam Hussein regime.

FBI

J. Edgar Hoover

J. Edgar Hoover served as head of the U.S. Federal Bureau of Investigation (FBI) for 48 years. Hoover was in charge of the FBI during a period when it was given wide powers to collect information on criminals and threats to national security inside U.S. borders.

Hoover used the FBI's intelligence sources to collect files of damaging information on important politicians throughout the United States. He kept many of these files under his personal control and used the details to influence governments and politicians.

The heads of intelligence organizations often carry much influence in government, and some senior figures in intelligence organizations become important politicians. For example, the President of Russia, Vladimir Putin, was a senior member of the KGB intelligence agency. George Bush Sr. was appointed Director of the U.S. Central Intelligence Agency (CIA) in 1976. Thirteen years later, he was elected president of the United States.

A shepherd ushers his sheep through an Iraqi village, past patrolling soldiers. Ordinary Iraqis, such as the shepherd, were directly affected by the espionage that led to the Iraq invasion.

Cuban missile crisis

In 1962 U.S. intelligence, including aerial photographs from U2 spy planes, revealed Soviet missile bases being constructed on the island of Cuba, only 120 miles from the U.S. mainland.

The U.S. government announced this information publicly and a period of heightened tension followed, during which public and government officials feared the outbreak of war.

Eventually, the Soviet Union withdrew the missiles, and the incident came to be known as the Cuban missile crisis.

Espionage in the modern world is a large industry employing thousands of people and costing billions of dollars. In most countries, the money spent by intelligence agencies is a closely guarded secret.

In the United States in 1997, this secret was partly revealed when the U.S. Congress was told by the head of the CIA, one of its major intelligence organizations, that total U.S. intelligence spending for the previous year was $26.6 billion.

Counter-intelligence

Counterintelligence is work performed to protect secrets from being uncovered and stolen by rivals and enemies. Counter-intelligence agencies monitor breaches in their security systems and search for enemy spies.

MRBM LAUNCH SITE 2
SAN CRISTOBAL
1 NOVEMBER 1962

MISSILE-READY TENT

FUEL TRAILERS

FORMER LAUNCH POSITIONS

FORMER LOCATION OF MISSILE-READY TENTS

Intelligence photographs detected the Soviet missile sites under construction in Cuba during 1962.

Why are such large sums of money spent? A large part of the answer comes from a country's desire to protect itself. Governments tend to publicize the fact that espionage is necessary for national security. Espionage can provide intelligence that determines where threats exist to national security and how serious those threats are. It can determine the types and number and location of weapons another country or group has. It can sometimes also discover what intentions a country or group has and whether they are planning an attack or invasion.

Much espionage work is performed to learn more about the intelligence organizations of other nations, how they operate, and what information they are seeking. Espionage is also performed to uncover plots and enemy spies working in a country, and to place secret agents in another country's intelligence organizations. The results of espionage by one nation can sometimes persuade its own government to take a certain course of action.

But some espionage missions can be designed to influence another country's government or people. From the end of World War II until the early 1990s, many countries of the world aligned themselves with one of the two superpowers: the United States and the Soviet Union. The world's two most powerful nations were hostile to and suspicious of each other but never fought against each other.

U.S. President John F. Kennedy (right) and Soviet Union President Nikita Khrushchev meet in the United States. Tensions between the two men subsequently reached their peak with the Cuban missile crisis of 1962.

Oleg Penkovsky

Oleg Penkovsky was a military intelligence officer in the Soviet Union who passed vital military secrets to the United States and Great Britain for 16 months during the early 1960s.

Before his capture and execution by the Soviets, Penkovsky revealed information regarding the Soviet forces, including details of their missiles. This information proved crucial to President John F. Kennedy during the Cuban missile crisis.

This period is known as the Cold War and saw both sides build up their weapons and military forces as well as creating the largest espionage networks the world had ever seen.

Influencing other nations

In the South American nation of Chile, for example, the CIA performed a series of espionage actions aimed to help remove President Allende from power. Allende was a left-wing leader whose policies were at odds with the U.S. government and there were fears for U.S. business interests in the country. Money was channeled to Allende's political opponents while the CIA kept Chile's military leaders unhappy with disinformation that they were to lose control of the armed forces. In 1973, members of the Chilean military led a coup, taking over the government, and General Agusto Pinochet became the leader of Chile.

The cost of industrial espionage

A 1999 survey conducted by an accountancy company, PriceWaterhouseCoopers, and the American Society for Industrial Security (ASIS), revealed that the top 1,000 companies in the United States lost more than $45 billion due to theft of information.

Chip espionage

In 2001, Say Lye Ow, a former employee of the U.S. computer chip manufacturer, Intel, was found guilty of copying designs of an advanced Itanium microprocessor. He was sentenced to two years in prison under the U.S. Economic Espionage Act of 1996.

Scientific and industrial espionage

Espionage is also used by countries to steal scientific and technological secrets from other nations. This work is performed to learn how much progress a rival nation has made as well as to help the stealing country's own technical programs.

In the years during and after World War II, the Soviet Union managed to place spies inside the Manhattan Project, the American program to build atomic bombs. A number of spies, including Klaus Fuchs, Ted Hall, and Julius and Ethel Rosenberg, learned details of how the technology worked. In 1949, the Soviet Union exploded their first atomic bomb and became the second nation with nuclear weapons technology. It is estimated that the espionage efforts of those spies saved Soviet scientists between two and eight years of research.

Industrial espionage (also known as commercial espionage) is the practice of spying on companies or organizations to learn what new products, innovations, and plans they have for their business. The spying can be performed by an individual, another company, or a nation.

Stealing technical and commercial secrets can save many years of research and development. During the 1960s, for example, a race developed to build the first airliner capable of flying at supersonic speeds (faster than the speed of sound). The Soviet intelligence organization, the KGB, placed secret agents in France who, along with Great Britain, were building the Concorde, which was more advanced than the Soviet airliner, TU-144. One of the Soviet agents, Sergei Fabiew, supplied the Soviet Union with a complete set of blueprints for Concorde. The TU-144 first flew at the end of 1968, beating Concorde's first flight by two months.

Agents of the KGB succeeded in obtaining complete plans for the Anglo-French Concorde (above) that resulted in the Soviet Union building a similar supersonic aircraft, the Tupolev TU-144.

Organizations & People

The United States has more intelligence organizations than any other country. The three most important intelligence agencies are the Central Intelligence Agency (CIA), the National Security Agency (NSA), and the Federal Bureau of Investigation (FBI). Although each organization's workload is varied and can overlap, in simple terms, the CIA is mainly concerned with espionage and intelligence-gathering abroad, the FBI is a crime-fighting and security force inside the United States, and the NSA is responsible for code-making (cryptography) and collecting and securing communications.

A boat from the U.S. Coast Guard, part of the Department of Homeland Security, escorts the liner Queen Mary 2 at St. Thomas in the U.S. Virgin Islands.

Department of Homeland Security

In 2003, in response to the attacks by terrorists on September 11, 2001, the first new U.S. government department since 1989 was created to counter the increased threat of terrorism in the United States. Named the Department of Homeland Security (DHS), it draws together an estimated 170,000 staff members from 22 different organizations.

A coding machine developed in the 19th century.

A coding machine developed in the 19th century.

In addition, the National Reconnaissance Office (NRO) co-ordinates the collection and analysis of information from missions flown by U.S. spy planes and satellites orbiting the Earth.

The CIA has its roots in World War II. Within six months of America's entry into the war in 1941, the Office of Strategic Services (OSS) was created to gather intelligence on, support, and carry out missions with resistance workers in Europe and Asia against German and Japanese forces. The CIA grew from the OSS and was officially founded in 1947. It is divided into four sections known as directorates: Administration, Science and Technology, Intelligence, and Operations. The CIA has had many notable successes, such as gaining information from high-level military figures in the Soviet Union and running disinformation campaigns to discredit and topple governments in Central and South America. It has also come under severe criticism, most recently in the aftermath of the September 11 terrorist attacks, for failing to protect against and warn of such attacks.

Codes & their purpose

All governments, intelligence organizations, and military forces require secrecy when sending certain messages. These could be a top secret order to an agent under cover in a hostile country, or a message conveying movement and target locations to a military force.

Codes are secret languages used to disguise the real meaning of a message by replacing words, letters, or whole sentences with different letters, numbers, or symbols. Unless the opposing force knows the code, they are unlikely to be able to unlock the true meaning of the message they have intercepted.

The CIA was criticized for failing to protect against the attacks of September 11, 2001, including that on the Pentagon in Virginia., shown here.

The KGB

The CIA's main adversary during the Cold War was the Soviet Union's Committee for State Security, better known by its Russian-language initials, the KGB. At its peak during the Cold War, the KGB employed an estimated 100,000 full-time personnel. Its influence was far-reaching, and it had the power to conduct espionage campaigns inside and outside of the Soviet Union. It successfully placed spies in governments and espionage agencies of enemy countries, such as Aldrich Ames in the United States and the Cambridge Spies in the United Kingdom. The KGB also worked closely with and influenced the intelligence agencies of its allies, such as the Stasi of East Germany, the StB of Czechoslovakia, and Bulgaria's Drzavna Segurnost (State Security) service.

Murder by umbrella

A Bulgarian espionage mission to assassinate Georgi Markov, a critic of the Bulgarian government, used an umbrella capable of injecting the lethal poison, ricin. The umbrella weapon was created in a KGB lab in Moscow and was used to murder Markov in London in 1978.

With the break-up of the Soviet Union in 1991, the KGB ceased to exist. However, in Russia (the largest and most powerful of the former Soviet republics), the task of performing espionage and disinformation abroad, and many of the KGB's contacts and spies, passed to a new organization, the SVR. The head of the SVR, believed to command as many as 15,000 staff, reports directly to the president of Russia.

Australian and British intelligence

In Australia and Great Britain there are twin agencies, one concerned with intelligence and security inside the country (Australian Security Intelligence Organization (ASIO) and Britain's MI5) and one that concentrates on gathering intelligence and performing espionage abroad (Australian Secret Intelligence Service (ASIS) and Britain's MI6).

Intelligence head

The head of the CIA has the title Director of the Central Intelligence Agency (DCIA). Before April 21, 2005, the DCIA was not only the head of the CIA but also the leader of the entire U.S. Intelligence Community, as the Director of Central Intelligence. He was the president's principal adviser on intelligence matters until the position of Director of National Intelligence was created after recommendations following the terrorist attacks on September 11, 2001.

The headquarters of MI6, Britain's international intelligence service, at Vauxhall Cross, London, on the banks of the River Thames.

Israel has five key intelligence agencies, of which Mossad (short for Central Institute for Intelligence and Security, in the Hebrew language) is the most important. Mossad was founded in 1951 and has carried out many undercover operations abroad. Mossad agents succeeded in kidnapping the former Nazi official Adolf Eichmann from Argentina to bring him to trial in Israel for war crimes, and have also assassinated a number of people, particularly members of the Palestine Liberation Organization (PLO).

Computers are vital research tools for people in all intelligence services.

MI5 and MI6 developed from the Secret Service Bureau, which was founded in 1909. While it is known that MI5 employs more than 2,200 people, almost half of whom are women, MI6's work abroad is shrouded in secrecy. Its existence was only officially admitted in 1994. Recent articles and a book by former MI6 officer Richard Tomlinson allege that MI6 has performed industrial espionage, delivering valuable secrets to British companies stolen from foreign competitors.

Wrong target

In 1974, Mossad agents in Norway carried out a mission to assassinate Ali Ahmad Salameh, the PLO figure believed to be responsible for the murder of Israeli athletes at the 1972 Olympic games. However, they misidentified their target and killed an Algerian waiter named Ahmad Bouchiki.

Five Mossad agents were arrested and sentenced to prison by the Norwegian authorities. In 1996, the Israeli government finally agreed to compensate Bouchiki's family.

People at work

The world's intelligence and espionage organizations employ thousands of people. Most of these work in offices and facilities in their home country where they assist in the process of gathering, analyzing, and reporting on intelligence. This is known as the intelligence cycle. It requires many people to decide what intelligence is needed, to plan how it can be obtained, and then analyze the recovered intelligence to produce reports.

Prime Minister Tony Blair with U.S. Defense Secretary Donald Rumsfeld, at Number 10 Downing Street.

Defecting to Moscow

Former CIA worker Edward Lee Howard defected to the Soviet Union in 1985. He was betrayed by a Soviet defector to the United States, Vitaly Yurchenko, who informed the CIA of a likely spy in their organization.

Howard's house was placed under constant observation and his car was often followed. Finally, Howard jumped out of a car driven by his wife; a dummy created to look like him took his place in the passenger seat. The trick gave him enough time to board a flight from the United States to Europe.

The "dodgy" dossier

Gathering intelligence from open sources is not without risk, as the British government discovered in 2002 when compiling a dossier of reports on Iraq and its forces.

Much of the report turned out to be copied from the work of a Californian student, Ibrahim al-Marashi. This created political uproar and caused serious problems for British Prime Minister Tony Blair.

Operation Mincemeat

Operation Mincemeat was a World War II British disinformation mission. The body of a warehouse worker who had died was planted on a shoreline in German territory with the false identity of Major Martin.

Documents on the body led the Germans to believe that Great Britain and its allies were planning to invade Greece when they actually planned to invade Sicily and then Italy. Large numbers of German troops were moved to Greece, helping to make the allied invasion of Italy a success.

Ensuring that intelligence is accurate is a vital part of the work of intelligence agencies. Important decisions, some of which may lead to the loss of life, may be made based upon intelligence. Large numbers of specialists are employed in intelligence agencies, from translators and linguists to experts in one region of the world or one type of religious or cultural group. Others are involved in computing or are analysts in a specialized technical field such as missile systems or chemical weapons. Agencies also employ skilled technicians in jobs such as mechanical and electrical engineering, printing, and tailoring to provide specialized equipment to spies.

Defectors, moles, double agents, and sleepers

Secret agents or spies are relatively small in number but perform crucial espionage work. There are a number of different types of agents at work in espionage.

Passing secrets to China

Larry Wu Tai Chin worked in the CIA from 1952 until he retired in 1981. During most of that time he worked as a mole for China, passing on secrets including the whereabouts of Chinese prisoners held captive in South Korea.

In the world of espionage it is vital that people are able to travel from country to country without attracting attention.

Many, such as couriers (who transport messages or equipment) and assassins, are classified by the job that they do. Other agents are classified by the nature of their role and who they work for. A defector, for example, is a person who leaves their home country to serve the interests of another country. Defectors from intelligence agencies are highly valued since they can be a vital source of secret information.

Moles are important agents who continue to work in a government, military, or intelligence service while passing secrets to another nation. America's most valuable known mole was a Soviet colonel, later promoted to general, named Dmitri Polyakov. He supplied information to the FBI and CIA for more than 20 years, revealing military secrets and identifying more than a dozen Soviet spies working in the United States. In 1986, he was captured and executed in the Soviet Union. It is believed that he was betrayed by Aldrich Ames, a mole working in the CIA who passed secrets to the KGB.

Opportunity lost

In 2003, a Somali-born computer student, Mohammed Warsame, was arrested on suspicion of aiding al-Qaeda, the terrorist group led by Osama Bin Laden.

The U.S. authorities planned to use Warsame as a double agent to infiltrate al-Qaeda to gain vital intelligence in the fight against terrorism. But Warsame's arrest and identity was leaked to the media, making the task no longer possible.

The Berlin tunnel

One of the most audacious CIA operations involved digging a 400-yard long tunnel under the city of Berlin in the 1950s to tap directly into East German telephone and other communication lines. The tunnel operated for many months and contained hundreds of tape recorders recording 1,200 hours of material every day.

A double agent is a spy engaged in secret activities for two or more intelligence services, providing information about one service to another. A double agent pretends that he is still loyal to his original agency while actually spying on them or feeding disinformation to them. During World War II, for example, the Spanish double agent Juan Pujol worked for both the German and the British intelligence forces. Pujol received the coveted Iron Cross medal from the Germans for the secrets he appeared to obtain from Great Britain. In reality, he was working for the British and feeding the Germans disinformation.

Sleepers are spies who move to a new country but may not start spying for many years. They take everyday jobs, become part of the community, and await contact and activation. Sleepers were used extensively by the KGB and its allies during the Cold War.

Gunter Guillaume is the most successful known sleeper: he arrived in West Germany during the 1950s and entered politics. In 1970 he was appointed as a personal advisor to Willy Brandt, the leader of West Germany, and after being activated as a spy, met world leaders and sat in on crucial meetings.

The Falcon and the Snowman

Christopher Boyce worked at TRW, a U.S. company that designed advanced spy satellite technology. He obtained many technical secrets and passed them to his friend, Andrew Daulton Lee, who sold them to the KGB. Captured and imprisoned in 1977, the pair's story was dramatized in the film *The Falcon and the Snowman*, which starred Sean Penn (left) and Timothy Hutton.

Antipodean espionage

In 1954 Vladimir Petrov, intelligence officer in the Soviet embassy in Australia, defected. Embassy officials made a clumsy effort to sneak his wife Evdokia back to Moscow. Anti-communist crowds at Sydney Airport tried to stop them; however, the BOAC flight took off for Darwin. There, officials convinced Mrs. Petrov she should defect as well.

He read secret messages from U.S. President Richard Nixon and vital reports about West Germany's military forces. He passed information back to East Germany for four years. When he was arrested in 1974, the scandal forced Brandt to resign as West German leader.

A spy's motivations

Spies caught and found guilty of acts of espionage face long periods in prison. In the past and in a handful of countries today, spies who are caught may even face death. So, why do spies risk all in order to spy?

Money is a powerful motivator for many spies. The prospect of personal wealth or the cancellation of personal debts has led many individuals into a life of espionage.

U.S. spy database

An espionage database is maintained by the Defense Personnel Security Research Center (PERSEREC) that contains statistics on 150 cases of espionage committed by U.S. citizens in the past 50 years. Ninety-three percent were men and over half of the female spies were recruited by their husband or boyfriend. Money was the key motivating factor in over 55 percent of cases, ideology the key in 22 percent.

Cruising the river in boats – known as punts – is a favorite recreation for students and visitors at Cambridge University.

Cambridge spies

The Cambridge Spies, so named because they attended Britain's Cambridge University, were supporters of communism and were easily recruited to work for the Soviet Union in the 1930s.

Guy Burgess, Donald Maclean, Anthony Blunt, and Kim Philby managed to secure important positions in the British government and intelligence agencies, where they obtained important secrets for the Soviets.

CIA employee Aldrich Ames volunteered his services to the KGB in 1985 in return for payment. When he was arrested and captured nine years later, Ames was estimated to have received cash and gifts with a total value of $2.7 million.

Ideology refers to the beliefs a person holds. Many spies choose to spy for countries whose views they agree with or against countries they disagree with.

An espionage organization may use force, the threat of imprisonment, or blackmail to convince someone to spy for them. This is referred to as compromise. Alfred Frenzel is one example of a person blackmailed into spying for an espionage organization.

Some agencies attract spies by flattering them and appealing to their sense of adventure or the idea that espionage is glamorous and exciting. These agencies play upon a spy's ego.

For a number of agents, it is a question of ideology. Many agents, especially in wartime, spy for their country in the belief that they are simply doing their patriotic duty. Other spies are motivated because

M-I-C-E

The reasons for people becoming and staying spies are often reduced to the acronym, M.I.C.E. This stands for Money, Ideology, Compromise, and Ego. Often, one or more of these is a factor in someone becoming a spy.

they are disillusioned or unhappy with their country, or work for countries who share their religious or political beliefs.

In the 1980s, Jonathan Pollard was a civilian working in intelligence for the U.S. Navy. He sympathized with Israel and the Jewish people and supplied Israel with information he believed was vital to that country's security. Pollard had high-level access to sensitive information and gave Israel over 800 files, including data on chemical weapons and other arms held by Israel's Arab neighbors in the Middle East. Pollard was caught and sentenced to life in prison, the longest sentence ever given to a U.S. spy for passing secrets to a friendly nation.

Targets

For espionage and disinformation to be successful, intelligence agencies need to carefully target their work. Sometimes, in the case of disinformation aimed at the general public of another nation, the target can be large. On other occasions, such as trying to recruit a high-ranking military officer to spy on his own forces, the target can be a single person.

Targeting new spies

The intelligence cycle starts with governments and intelligence agencies deciding exactly what vital information they wish to learn and how this information can be obtained. Intelligence agencies identify people who may have access to this information and target them for recruitment. These targets range from officers in intelligence organizations or military forces to people in seemingly ordinary jobs such as janitors, valets, and chauffeurs.

Intelligence officers have varying skills and experiences, depending on the jobs they are required to do by the service that has recruited them.

When recruiting new officers as spies, agencies may use money, flattery, and appeals to the person's ego to persuade them to spy. On a number of occasions, darker tactics are used. Some people have been tricked, forced, or blackmailed into becoming spies. Sometimes, targets have been lured into a blackmail situation, often tricked into a sexual act or committing a crime that is held over them as a threat. On other occasions, thorough background checks into a potential target's history and lifestyle reveal facts that can be used to force the target into spying.

Alfred Frenzel was a senior politician in West Germany who was blackmailed by Czechoslovakian intelligence agents. After discovering information of his past life in Czechoslovakia, they threatened to reveal his criminal record and membership of the Communist Party unless he passed on secrets. Fearing the end of his political career, Frenzel became an important spy for the Czechs. He passed on a complete copy of West Germany's defense budget as well as top secret details of new missiles and aircraft.

Walk-ins

A walk-in is a person who makes the first move and volunteers their services to an intelligence agency. Many spies, such as Aldrich Ames and Jonathan Pollard, were walk-ins.

Targeting leaders

The leaders of nations have often been the target of espionage or disinformation missions. Disinformation campaigns aimed at a country's ruler may try to discredit them in the eyes of their government or their allies, or to influence them into carrying out a particular action.

In the 1960s, the rival superpowers battled over influence in the Asian nation of Indonesia. The United States gave millions of dollars in aid and recognized Indonesia's claim to Dutch West Guinea. In 1964, the Czech StB, helped by the KGB, launched a disinformation campaign against Sukarno, the Indonesian president. The goal was to turn him away from U.S. influence. Informers met with senior members of the Indonesian government and showed forged documents that detailed a British and U.S. plan to invade Indonesia and a CIA plot to assassinate the president.

President Sukarno of Indonesia, who was persuaded to take an anti-American stance by Soviet and Czech intelligence operatives in 1964.

Valet turned spy

Elyesa Bazna was an Albanian who spied for Germany during World War II. Working as a valet for the British ambassador in Turkey, Bazna managed to crack safes and locked document boxes and take photographs of top secret documents that showed how Great Britain was attempting to lure Turkey into the war on the side of the allied forces.

Young people confront military police during an anti-Vietnam War demonstration at Arlington, Virginia, in 1967.

Neither plot was true, but the evidence was convincing. Sukarno took an anti-U.S. stance that was publicized by newspapers. Anti-U.S. feeling in the country increased and many of the close ties with the United States were broken.

On other occasions, acts of espionage try not to influence a leader but to assassinate them. Assassination attempts by intelligence agencies have occurred throughout history. Many have been unsuccessful, such as the attempts on the life of Adolf Hitler, leader of Nazi Germany, and Fidel Castro, president of Cuba, and British and French attempts to assassinate President Gemal Nasser of Egypt during the 1950s.

Discrediting Castro and Cuba

During the 1960s, the CIA considered plans to launch disinformation blaming Cuba for things it had not actually done. The idea was to provide international agreement and acceptance for a U.S. invasion of Cuba. The plans included Operation Bingo, a fake attack on a U.S. naval base, and Operation Dirty Trick, in which a space launch would appear to fail due to Cuban efforts. Neither plan was actually carried out.

In more recent times, plans have been made to assassinate the leader of al-Qaeda, Osama Bin Laden, as well as other leaders of terrorist groups. In 1996, for example, Yehiya Ayyash, known as "The Engineer" for his expert bomb-making for the Palestinian group, Hamas, was assassinated. An explosive device was planted inside his mobile phone and detonated when the phone rang. The Israeli espionage services have been accused of the assassination, but it remains unproven who ordered the mission.

Deadly lips – a pistol contained within what appears to be lipstick.

Targeting dissidents

Dissidents are people who disagree with and criticize the government of a country or its policies. In many countries, such critics are tolerated as part of the process of freedom of speech that allows people to hold and express their personal opinions. But in many countries, some political groups or dissidents are closely watched by intelligence agencies, who might listen in on telephone conversations and monitor who they meet using surveillance techniques.

Former assassin becomes the target

Spies who give up their trade or switch sides can become key targets for assassination. In 1954, Nicolai Khokhlov, a KGB assassin, was sent into West Germany with orders to kill the dissident, Georgi Okolovich. Khokhlov didn't perform his mission. Instead, he defected and warned Okolovich of the threats against him. Three years later, the KGB poisoned their ex-assassin with a radioactive substance called thallium. Only a series of blood transfusions enabled Khokhlov to survive.

In the Soviet Union and Eastern Europe during the Cold War, many dissidents were imprisoned and some were even assassinated. The KGB agent Bogdan Stashinsky defected in 1961 and revealed chilling secrets of his trade as an assassin. He had been trained in 1957 to use a gun that fired a poisonous gas that triggered a heart attack in its target, making the victim appear to die of natural causes. Stashinsky testified that he used a similar weapon to kill two dissidents, Lev Rebet and Stefan Bandera.

Provocateurs

A provocateur is an agent, usually working for an intelligence agency, who joins a political organization or group not just to provide information on its members, but to stir them into often violent action. The group's actions can then be used by the intelligence agency to trap or discredit the group.

Robotic assassination

In South Yemen in 2002, a remote-controlled flying robot called a Predator UAV attacked a vehicle carrying senior al-Qaeda terrorist Sinan al-Harethi and five other al-Qaeda operatives. The CIA-controlled flying robot fired a Hellfire guided missile, killing all six suspected terrorists.

The KGB exploited racial tension in the United States to generate anti-American sentiments in African countries.

Targeting the foreign public

The general public of foreign nations have often been the target of disinformation campaigns. Until the break-up of the USSR in the early 1990s, much of the KGB's disinformation tried to discredit the United States in the eyes of the general public of other nations. The KGB leaked or circulated articles and news stories accompanied with forged letters and documents that appeared to prove that these stories were true. During the 1960s, for example, racial tensions were high in the United States.

Dissident groups are sometimes targeted for infiltration. This is when an agent joins a target group and, over time, strives to become a trusted member while feeding important information back to their intelligence agency. During the Vietnam War, the FBI and CIA worked together to infiltrate and spy on those people who protested against the war in the United States. The official goal of Operation Chaos, as the campaign was called, was to verify whether the anti-war movement was backed by a foreign government, especially hostile nations such as the Soviet Union. More than 13,000 people were investigated and files created on them and their activities. Approximately 7,200 of these people were U.S. citizens.

Poisoning the President

In 1960, the president of the African nation of Congo, Patrice Lumumba, sought military aid from the Soviet Union. The CIA was alarmed and targeted Lumumba for assassination. Local criminals were briefed and trained in the use of a kit of bacteria poison in neighboring Zaire. The plan, though, proved unworkable. Shortly afterward, Lumumba was murdered by political opponents inside Congo.

The KGB attempted to exploit this by feeding disinformation to targets in the United States and abroad. According to Oleg Kalugin, former KGB General, disinformation exaggerating racism in the United States was sent to African nations with large black populations to generate anti-U.S. feeling. The KGB also sent forged hate-mail to African diplomats at the United Nations, making it appear to be from white racists in the United States.

Olympics threat

The Soviet Union and its allies in Eastern Europe (except for Romania) boycotted the 1984 Summer Olympics in Los Angeles in protest of the U.S. boycott of the 1980 Moscow games.

The Soviets also circulated disinformation that a U.S. racist organization, the Ku Klux Klan, planned to kill African and Asian athletes at the 1984 Los Angeles Olympics. It was an attempt to influence other countries to boycott the games, but no African or Asian nation joined the boycott.

Operation Mass Appeal

Scott Ritter, a former United Nations chief weapons inspector, maintains that MI6, the British intelligence organization, ran a disinformation campaign in 1997 and 1998 to exaggerate the threat of weapons held in the Middle Eastern nation of Iraq. Ritter stated that the campaign, Operation Mass Appeal, was designed to "shake up public opinion" and increase support for a proposed attack or invasion.

Source: BBC News

A Long History

Espionage has occurred for thousands of years. Whenever there have been conflicts or rivalries between two different tribes, kingdoms, or other opposing forces, there have usually been people sent as scouts or spies to observe and gather information on the enemy.

The importance of espionage to the military was explained in detail by Chinese writer Sun Tzu in *The Art of War*. The oldest surviving copy of this work, written on strips of bamboo, is between 2,000 and 2,200 years old. Sun Tzu called spies the eyes and ears of an army, and theorized that all war is based on deception. He also explained ways of spreading disinformation through enemy forces.

One of the earliest known examples of disinformation occurred roughly 3,200 years ago during the reign of the Ancient Egyptian pharaoh, Ramses II. The Hittite city of Kadesh (located in modern-day Syria) was under threat of attack from a powerful Ancient Egyptian army. The Hittites sent two spies who were captured and brought before Ramses II for questioning. Appearing to be in fear, the two spies told the pharaoh the location of the Hittite army. But their information was deliberately false, and as a result, Ramses' army was lured into a trap and surrounded. Only the arrival of thousands more Egyptian soldiers prevented Ramses' forces from being crushed.

Caesar Cipher

Roman Emperor Julius Caesar invented his own code to send messages that, if intercepted by his enemies, would be unreadable. He moved each letter of the alphabet three places along so that *c* became *f*, *d* became *g* and so on. Shifting letters back or forth in the alphabet to make a code is now called the Caesar Cipher.

Espionage in the distant past may not have used cameras, bugs, and other technology available today, but many of the basic skills and techniques of spying were the same. Writing messages in code was common in the times of Ancient Egypt, Greece, and Rome, while techniques such as surveillance and disguise were also used. Counter-espionage and disinformation were also practiced during the time of Ancient Rome. As the Roman Empire grew in size, the threat to its leaders often came from within the empire.

Disinformation was a powerful weapon used by the leader of the Mongol Empire, Genghis Khan, in the 12th and 13th centuries. Khan built an enormous empire that stretched from China across Asia and into Europe.

He used spies to gather intelligence about his enemy's forces and also sent agents into enemy strongholds ahead of his troops to spread rumor and disinformation. These agents would act as local people who encouraged talk of the might of Genghis Khan and his violent army that could not be beaten. They spread disinformation that a quick surrender would mean riches and peace. As a result, many strongholds gave up the fight or became so divided in opinion that conquering them became easier.

Biblical spies

The Bible refers to an incident when Joshua, leader of the Israelite people, sent two spies into the walled city of Jericho, where they hid in a house of a woman called Rahab before reporting back to their commander. In the book of Numbers in the Bible, God also urges Moses to send agents to "spy out the lands of Canaan."

Spy networks

Most of the intelligence organizations in the modern world were created in the 20th century. However, organized spy rings or networks led by a spymaster existed many centuries earlier. From the 16th century onward, a number of countries in Europe developed organized networks of spies and informers. They were designed to report on intended plots to overthrow leaders as well as to gather secrets about alliances between enemy countries.

Sir Francis Walsingham, spymaster to Queen Elizabeth I of England, had a network of over 50 spies in the palaces and kingdoms of Europe, and established a department of code-breaking. His spies foiled numerous plots, although some may have been disinformation by Walsingham, designed to make himself appear more powerful and successful and to act as a warning to genuine conspirators.

Queen Elizabeth I made widespread use of espionage through her spymaster Sir Francis Walsingham.

Pompeius's plot

Roman Emperor Julius Caesar was the victim of a disinformation campaign instigated by his opponent, Pompeius, after losing the battle of Dyrrachium. Letters were sent by Pompeius to every Roman settlement to exaggerate the defeat, stating that Caesar's armies had been wiped out and that many trade routes were no longer safe. It turned out to be an unsuccessful attempt to remove Julius Caesar from power.

The Babington Plot

Mary Queen of Scots was jailed in Tudor England but was sent secret messages smuggled inside a beer barrel. Mary and an ally, Sir Anthony Babington, plotted to remove Queen Elizabeth I of England from power, but were unaware that the messenger who carried the barrel was a double agent. He worked for Queen Elizabeth's spymaster, Sir Francis Walsingham. The plot was foiled and both Mary and Babington were executed.

Mary Queen of Scots

In France, Cardinal Richelieu was chief advisor to King Louis XIII and the effective ruler of the country. He established the Cabinet Noir, considered the first official intelligence service, which kept watch on French aristocrats and frequently intercepted and read their letters and messages. Prussia rose to become a powerful state in Europe mainly during the reign of Frederick the Great, who installed a spy network believed to number close to a thousand agents.

Cardinal Richelieu of France, who established the world's first official intelligence organization

In the United States, espionage activities began in earnest during the Revolutionary War. In 1775, George Washington was appointed commander of the Continental Army fighting the British for independence. With fewer soldiers and poorer equipment than the British, Washington used espionage and disinformation wherever possible.

Washington's agents planted disinformation that frequently misled the British as to where his armies were located and planned to attack. For example, Washington used a double agent named James Rivington to convince the British that Washington planned to attack New York when, in fact, his armies joined French forces and fought the British at Yorktown, Virginia.

Civil War spies

The American Civil War (1861–1865) saw a great number of spies employed by both the Union forces of the northern states and the Confederate forces of the south. It was also the first major conflict in which photography was used as a tool of espionage. For example, photojournalist Alexander Gardner had access to the Confederate camps but was actually working for Union forces.

Deceiving the British

George Washington succeeded in spreading disinformation about the size of his armed forces. His assistant, Major John Clark, became skilled at leaking documents revealing the American army's size to the British.

The documents exaggerated Washington's forces, making them appear four or five times larger than they really were. The British, recognizing Washington's handwriting, believed them to be accurate.

George Washington

His photographs of soldiers were examined to find double agents. However, both sides relied on individuals to risk their lives to obtain vital information. Neither side had a truly organized intelligence service until near the war's end.

Many of the spies on both sides were women. Emma Edmonds, for example, was a Canadian-born Union spy who successfully disguised herself both as a white man and as a black slave to spy on Confederate troops. There were equally as many female spies on the Confederate side, including the sisters Lottie and Ginnie Moon, Belle Boyd, and society hostess Rose O'Neal Greenhow. The last set up a spy network in Washington that obtained the timetable of the Union Army's movements. This information proved vital, and contributed to the Confederate victory in the First Battle of Bull Run in 1861.

Jefferson Davis

Under cover

One account describes Union spies Elizabeth Van Lew and Mary Bowser, who successfully disguised Emma Edmonds as a black servant and placed her in the household of the Confederate leader, Jefferson Davis.

There, Edmonds posed as a slave who could neither read nor write and was ignored as Davis and important generals held meetings. Edmonds memorized conversations she overheard and documents that she gained access to, and passed this vital information back to Union generals.

Fact & Fiction

James Fenimore Cooper's 1821 book – a tale of espionage during the American Revolution – is the first spy novel in Western literature. Since that time, hundreds of thrillers and adventure stories featuring spies and spying have been published. A major boom in espionage stories occurred during the early part of the Cold War, when many writers, some of whom had served in intelligence organizations during World War II, began to write spy stories. Set in a Cold War world of intrigue, mystery, and danger, these stories made heroes out of fictional secret agents and captured the imagination of the public at the time. Many senior figures in intelligence agencies did nothing to stop this view since it offered a glamorous and positive image of their work. It also provided good publicity to organizations that could not publicize their real activities.

James Bond author Ian Fleming is seen here on the set of the first film, Dr. No, *with Sean Connery, who played the lead in seven James Bond films.*

Licensed to thrill?

No fictional spy has done more to boost the public image of espionage than James Bond. Over a third of the entire global population, more than two billion people, have seen one or more of the twenty official Bond movies. Tens of millions have read one or more of the many Bond books, and James Bond has become an icon in popular culture. The character first appeared in the 1950s in a series of books written by Ian Fleming. During World War II, Fleming had served as an intelligence officer in the British navy.

U.S. President John F. Kennedy revealed his fondness for Ian Fleming's James Bond novels in the early 1960s, and throughout that decade and beyond, the popularity of fictional spies boomed. Dozens of books and TV shows appeared, including the U.S. television series *Get Smart*, *I Spy* starring Bill Cosby, and *The Man from* U.N.C.L.E. Such shows depicted a similar world to

U.S. President John F. Kennedy revealed his enthusiasm for the James Bond books written by Ian Fleming.

the glamour of James Bond. But from the 1970s, writers began to show a less glamorous, more realistic view of spying in which victories were rare or small and there were no heroes, only agents on both sides trying to do their often tiring job. But popular films and TV shows especially have created and maintained a glamorous, action-packed image of spies and espionage. Many modern spy movies, from *Spy Kids* and *Mission Impossible* to the James Bond series, are full of chaotic and often violent fight scenes, impossible escapes, and marathon chases using every form of transportation imaginable. Espionage in real life tends to be quite different.

The real James Bond

Ian Fleming's Bond character was based on his own experiences and imagination. It was also based on the life of Yugoslav-born double agent, Dusan "Dusko" Popov. First recruited by the Germans, Popov worked for the British as a double agent during World War II and discovered secrets concerning the bombing of Pearl Harbor.

Edward Fox, in the film The Day of the Jackal, *playing the role of an assassin hired by the French OAS organization to kill President Charles de Gaulle. The story involved the frantic efforts of British and French intelligence groups to stop the assassination.*

Fact v. fiction

"Movie-makers love heroes and villains, clean endings, clear positions about right and wrong... so, most spy movies are glorified and unrealistic global cop films.**"**

James Grady,
writer of the spy novel
Six Days of the Condor

Very little spy work is truly action-packed. Almost all the people working for an intelligence agency deal with information. They try to obtain it, analyze it, understand it, and report back to others about it. Making important contacts and gathering vital information can take months, sometimes years, and patience is essential. Fictional spies in movies and on TV are often depicted as brave loners, working single-handedly to stop an evil villain from world domination. In reality, almost all spies work as part of a larger team. When a spy working in the field uncovers important information, their main goal is to convey that information back to their agency. Force is rarely used by agents in the field unless they are suddenly trapped. If the need arises for a kidnapping, an assassination, or a major break-in, specialists are usually called in.

A real spy operating under cover does everything within their power to keep their work secret. According to the former head of the CIA, William Colby, the perfect agent is "a gray man, so inconspicuous that he can never catch the waiter's eye in a restaurant." Out in the field, spies seek to blend in with their environment so they do not attract attention.

Unlike in movies, the identity of real-life spies is fiercely protected. For example, Markus Wolf was head of the East German secret service, the HVA, at the height of the Cold War. Yet for 20 years, no one in the West knew his identity and he was nicknamed "the man with no face."

Changing enemies

With the end of the Cold War, the traditional enemy used in Western spy stories, the Soviet Union and its allies, was no longer relevant. Recent movies, including the Jack Ryan series starring Harrison Ford, have used drug kingpins and terrorists as enemies.

The ideal spy can blend into the crowd and become part of the landscape wherever he or she is working.

Secret library

In the 1950s, the director of the CIA, Allen Dulles, provided fictional plot ideas to the well-known writer of espionage novels, Helen MacInnes. The CIA also created a library featuring many of the fictional spy novels and stories.

Espionage gadgets

One of the most popular elements of the fictional spy stories is the wide range of incredible gadgets used by the agents. In the James Bond films, these gadgets are supplied by Q, a character based on a real-life British technical innovator, Charles Fraser-Smith, who equipped resistance workers, prisoners of war, and spies during World War II. In the United States, Stanley Lovell was the head of the Research and Development Branch of the OSS, which developed explosives camouflaged as flour, hidden radio transmitters, and a range of small, secret guns and other weapons during World War II.

Many gadgets, such as James Bond's laser watch and, in *Die Another Day*, an Aston Martin car that could become invisible, are pure fantasy. Others, such as portable jet packs, cameras hidden inside neck-ties, and radio transmitters concealed

Operation Mongoose

Between 1961 and 1963, the CIA mounted Operation Mongoose to find ways of removing Fidel Castro as leader of Cuba. Plans considered included contaminating a box of Castro's favorite brand of cigars with lethal bacteria, and building an exploding seashell and placing it on the ocean floor in the area where Castro liked to scuba dive.

in shoe heels, do exist. Real-life espionage has produced many strange and surprising pieces of equipment. For example, listening devices were fitted inside artificial rocks and tree stumps, while the KGB's "Kiss of Death" was a lipstick tube turned into a single-shot weapon.

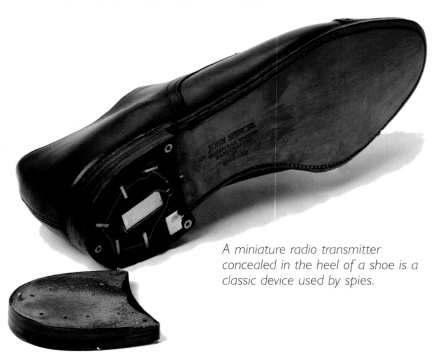

A miniature radio transmitter concealed in the heel of a shoe is a classic device used by spies.

EYE SPY

In the film *Mission Impossible*, cameras hidden in eyeglasses are used for spying. Such devices actually exist and, with the aid of a radio transmitter, can send images to a display screen some distance away.

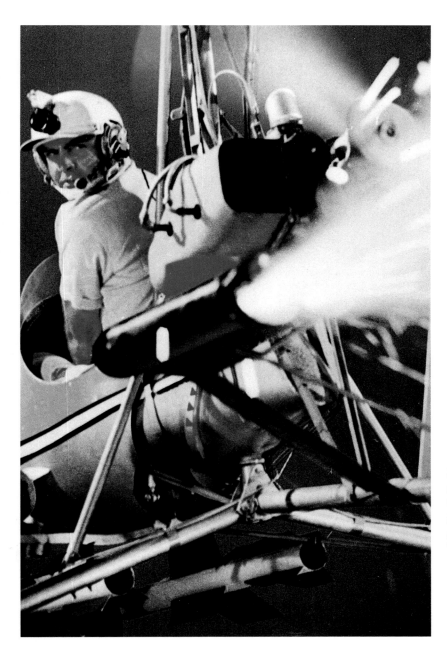

Sean Connery, playing James Bond, makes use of the weaponry in his "Little Nelly" helicopter to fight off an airborne attack in You Only Live Twice.

Espionage Techniques

Soviet photographs of the wreckage of Gary Powers' U2 aircraft, and the surveillance equipment it was carrying.

M ost espionage missions are concerned with identifying, collecting, and sending intelligence. This intelligence can be divided into a number of types based on how it can be collected. OSINT is open-source intelligence – sources of information that are freely available such as foreign newspapers, Internet websites, or radio broadcasts. HUMINT is human intelligence – the collection and processing of information from spies and informers, often working behind enemy lines. IMINT is imagery intelligence – the collection of photographs and other images, usually from aerial sources such as spy planes or satellites. SIGINT is signals intelligence – the interception and collection of information sent as signals, such as radio waves.

Spyplane shot down

The most celebrated case of aerial spying occurred in 1960 when a CIA U2 spy plane, piloted by Francis Gary Powers, was shot down over the Soviet Union. The U.S. government claimed that Powers had been performing a weather observation flight but, under questioning, Powers admitted spying. He was put on trial by the Soviet Union and imprisoned. Powers was released in exchange for a Soviet spy in 1962.

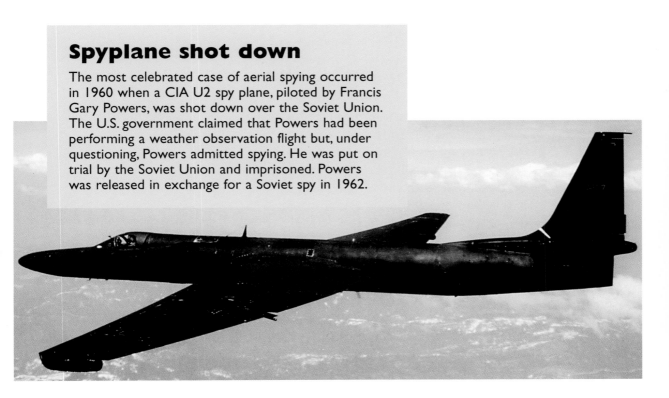

In espionage today, a wide variety of different techniques and technology are used to identify and collect each type of intelligence. For example, IMINT is collected by spy planes embarking on risky missions over enemy territory. These aircraft tend to be lightly armed, relying instead on their speed and flying at high altitudes to complete missions safely. Spy plane missions can also be performed at ground-hugging altitudes (below 300 yards) in order to take highly close-up photographs. These extremely dangerous missions are increasingly being performed with robotic devices called unmanned aerial vehicles (UAVs). During the 2003 invasion of Iraq, more than ten different types of UAV were used by the United States and its allies to provide intelligence on Iraqi troop positions and movements.

Zooming in

According to the Federation of American Scientists (FAS), three spy satellites operated by the U.S. National Reconnaissance Office (NRO) carry cameras with a resolution sharper than four inches. This means they are capable of spotting an object the size of an orange from as far as 180–250 miles away.

Spy satellites

More and more imagery intelligence is being collected by spy satellites. These are satellites orbiting Earth equipped with phenomenally powerful imaging systems. Spy satellites may be equipped with cameras to take photographs in visible light, or they may be equipped with radar instruments capable of capturing images through clouds or in darkness.

A U.S. Air Force SR-71 Blackbird spy aircraft, successor to the U2.

Spy satellites were first used by the superpowers in the 1960s. Since that time, the quality of the images they can obtain and their ability to zoom in on the Earth's surface has increased greatly. Spy satellites have the ability to spot troop movements on the ground and the construction of military facilities such as a missile launch site. They can also detect flying aircraft and moving road convoys, and track missiles in flight.

Other satellites are involved in the interception of intelligence signals. SIGINT satellites monitor signals sent as energy waves, which can include television and radio broadcasts, and telecommunications signals such as faxes. Information that is intercepted is known as chatter and can include phone calls from both land lines and mobile phones.

The Zimmermann telegram

Intelligence operations played a major role in the United States declaring war on Germany in World War I. In 1917 British intelligence forces intercepted a telegram from the German foreign minister, Arthur Zimmermann. It urged Mexico to declare war on the United States. The British passed the message on to the United States, who entered World War I shortly afterward.

A spy satellite in orbit around the Earth, one of many such vehicles providing surveillance from high altitudes.

FBI'S Magic Lantern

In 2002, news emerged of a computer program developed by the FBI that could record keystrokes. Named Magic Lantern, it could be delivered unknowingly to a person's computer, much like a computer virus, and send back details of the keystrokes to an FBI computer located elsewhere.

Although their exact abilities are shrouded in secrecy, it is believed that these satellites, working with computer-based systems on the ground, can capture and record chatter sent from electronic devices like phones, faxes, and radios. They then send messages to listening posts on Earth where they are transferred to powerful computer networks. These computers use advanced computer filtering software to analyze the content of messages and search for important intelligence. The software, it is believed, analyzes messages from particular targets, such as the phone line of a suspected terrorist, and searches for particular keywords that could reveal a location or a planned mission. Only a relatively small number of the

Project Echelon

Project Echelon is so secret that some of the nations believed to be involved in its operation have not publicly admitted its existence. According to the American Civil Liberties Union, the countries involved are the United States, the United Kingdom, Canada, Australia, and New Zealand.

It is believed to be the largest electronic monitoring system in the world and potentially capable of intercepting hundreds of millions of phone and possibly Internet messages every 24 hours.

hundreds of thousands or millions of messages searched by the computers will be studied by human intelligence officers. But sometimes, the results can be important. Intercepted phone calls, for example, led to the capture of a suspected al-Qaeda operative, Khalid Sheikh Mohammed, in March 2003.

Intelligence-gathering techniques also target computers. Many computers are linked to networks or the Internet, the largest computer network of all. This can enable an intelligence agency equipped with the right computer hardware and software to access another computer's files without the user knowing. Computers used by targets such as suspected spies, criminals, or terrorists are sometimes fitted with devices called keystroke recorders. These log every press of the keyboard and can replay thousands of previous keystrokes in order to reveal typed messages, documents, or computer passwords.

A powerful ground station capable of receiving signals from spy satellites in orbit over the Earth.

Surveillance and eavesdropping

Surveillance is the technique of observing people or places over a period of time. Intelligence agencies target a range of different people, from criminals to dissidents, as well as people suspected to be enemy spies. Surveillance staff work together as a team and may include agents in a stakeout location across from or close to a target building, and specialized drivers trained to keep track of a moving vehicle without being detected.

Stasi surveillance

At its height during the Cold War, the East German secret service, the Stasi, conducted thousands of surveillance operations every year. It had a staff of close to 100,000 people, a network of close to half a million informers, and files on roughly a third of the country's population – more than 5 million people.

Berlin's majestic Brandenburg Gate epitomized the world of espionage for 40 years. Until the collapse of the Communist regimes in eastern Europe, it was a high-profile checkpoint for people and vehicles crossing the Berlin Wall.

Surveillance teams use powerful cameras, night vision goggles, and thermal imagers that create pictures by detecting a build-up of heat. This can show people, vehicles, and other equipment. Other photographic equipment is designed to be easily concealed inside bags, behind a suit tie, or hidden inside a belt buckle, umbrella handle, or cigarette case.

In 2000 and 2001, the FBI conducted surveillance operations against one of its own agents, Robert Hanssen. Intelligence from the CIA suggested that Hanssen was a spy for the SVR, the successor to the KGB. Hanssen was appointed to a new job at FBI headquarters so that he could be monitored more effectively. The FBI bought the house across from his own home in Vienna, Virginia, and conducted lengthy surveillance operations. Hanssen's phone was tapped and his car fitted with bugs.

Bugging in Moscow

A wooden replica of the Great Seal of the United States was given as a gift from the Soviet Union to the U.S. Ambassador to Moscow. It was hung on the wall of the Ambassador's office for six years before its real purpose was detected.

Hidden inside the seal was a bug capable of transmitting secret conversations to a receiver located in a van parked outside the embassy.

Requesting phone taps

Telephone tapping is strictly controlled in most countries. Police forces and intelligence agencies often have to apply to a court to gain permission to perform taps. In 2002, courts granted the U.S. government 1,228 requests to perform secret telephone taps and/or searches of homes of suspected spies and terrorists.

His personal computer was also secretly searched without his knowledge. In February 2001, FBI surveillance teams tracked Hanssen as he drove to Foxstone Park in Virginia and dropped off a bag containing secret FBI files and computer disks. It was revealed that Hanssen had spied for the KGB and the SVR for more than 10 years.

Surveillance is often used as a technique in conjunction with eavesdropping, which is literally listening in on people's conversations. Eavesdropping can sometimes mean placing a person within earshot of an important conversation. For example, Emma Edmonds posed as an innocent-appearing servant at the home of Jefferson Davis, leader of the Confederate forces during the American Civil War. She was present at important meetings and was able to pass on much valuable intelligence.

In modern-day espionage, eavesdropping tends to mean the use of electronic hardware. Directional microphones, for example, can be pointed in the direction of a room or location and pick up sound from more than 100 yards away. Small digital voice recorders can be hidden inside everyday objects and left to record hours of conversations, only to be secretly collected later.

The famous German Enigma coding machine whose secrets were finally broken after an intensive effort during World War II, by technicians at Britain's Government Communications Headquarters, Bletchley Park.

Native American code

An unusual code system used by the U.S. Marines during World War II was based on the unwritten language of the Native American Navajo people. Over 370 Navajo Code Talkers served with the U.S. Marines and relayed messages via radios or telephone. The code was never broken.

Bugs are the most common of all electronic eavesdropping devices. These are usually small devices containing a microphone that collects sound from the immediate area, and a transmitter that can send the sound using radio waves to a receiver located some distance away. Bugs can be made small enough to be fitted inside many different everyday objects such as watches, electrical plugs, and pens. Telephone taps, sometimes known as wiretaps, are a type of bug used to record telephone conversations, usually without the caller's knowledge.

Keeping secrets

While many techniques and much technology is used to gather intelligence, an almost equal effort is made to protect intelligence once it is obtained. Every nation has organizations responsible for the protection of its secret data and communications. Counter-surveillance teams in intelligence agencies may use special scanners and other equipment to "sweep" a room to try to detect bugs, miniature video cameras, and other espionage devices.

Microdots

Microdot photography can reduce a whole page of a letter-sized document down to the size of a period. At this incredibly small size, microdots can be hidden in almost any item, but require a special viewer in order to be read.

A mobile satellite communications unit used by the U.S. Army in the field.

Their goal is to create a safe environment for top secret meetings and work to take place. Counter-espionage teams are on a constant search to locate and hunt down enemy spies and informers who may reveal secrets. Agents out in the field who fear they are under surveillance may use escape techniques or disguises in order to shake off the people who are tracking their moves.

Protecting information by using secret codes has a long history, and made great advances during World War II when some of the earliest computers were built to make or break codes. Today, extremely powerful supercomputers are at work in organizations such as the

NSA and Britain's Government Communications Headquarters (GCHQ) dedicated to cryptography – the science of making secure codes that cannot be broken.

Getting messages back

Once secret agents have obtained vital data, they must send this data back to their intelligence organization without being detected. Many different methods can be used. Couriers are people who transport secret information or equipment between secret agents and their intelligence organization. They may never meet the agent, instead using a dead drop site. This is a place agreed upon in advance, where two

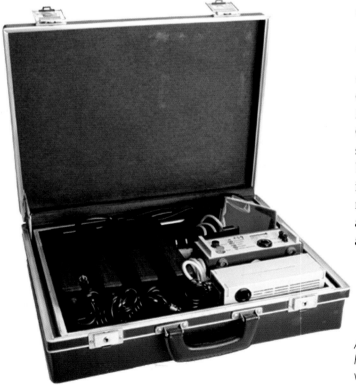

A special kit developed to detect hidden or invisible writing on a variety of surfaces.

or more people visit at different times, never being seen together. Messages can be written in code, written using invisible ink, or hidden in a picture that when washed with certain chemicals reveals the real message. Many secrets have been passed from one person to another concealed in all types of items, from documents stuffed inside jars of baby food to rolls of film fitted inside a hollowed-out bolt.

Disinformation techniques

Disinformation must reach its audience in a way that makes the audience believe it may be, or is, true. Disinformation targeted at senior figures in governments or the military is often delivered by a well-regarded agent, who is actually a double agent, working for the other side. Often, disinformation is backed up with forged documents and statements that appear to reinforce the truthfulness of the disinformation.

An extremely common technique is to accompany well-known true statements with false ones, so that on receiving the disinformation, the audience knows that some of the story is true, and is more likely to accept that the rest of the message is accurate as well.

Much disinformation, sent by intelligence agencies to influence public opinion, plays on the public's prejudices and fears. False stories or

Three KGB atrocity stories

The KGB used disinformation including the following false stories to provoke anti-American feeling in other countries or to stir up unrest among minority, religious, or racial groups in the United States:

The CIA was behind the 1981 assassination attempt on Pope John Paul II.

The United States developed an "ethnic weapon" able to kill black people but to spare white people. In the Middle East, a similar campaign suggested that the U.S. would kill Arabs and not kill Jewish people.

The U.S. stole babies from less developed nations to use their organs for transplant.

Source: *The CNN Cold War Experience*

claims that reflect very negatively on an enemy target are called atrocity stories. During World War I, an atrocity story circulated in Great Britain about the Germans and their use of a "corpse-conversion factory" that turned dead soldiers' bodies into soap. There was no truth in the story, but as the Germans became feared opponents during World War II, many people believed it to be true and the myth lasted for many years.

Understanding Espionage

The role, technique, and targets of espionage have changed greatly in recent times. Billions of pieces of information are communicated around the world every day. The result has been that the majority of intelligence is gathered not by human spies but by technology such as computers. The targets of espionage and disinformation have changed as well; although traditional rivals such as the United States and Russia still spy on each other, the distinction between friendly nation and foe has become blurred. Espionage and disinformation activities may be carried out in nations considered friendly in general but who differ from another country on just one issue.

U.S. Coast Guard personnel with suspected pirates apprehended in the Arabian Gulf. The Coast Guard, part of the Department of Homeland Security, reacts to intelligence reports on enemy activities within the region.

The Royal Air Force base at Menwith Hill, England. The domes house radar units used in covert surveillance work for intelligence agencies.

The need for security

Most governments maintain that the need for intelligence and secrecy is more important today than in the past. They say that the threats to national security today are harder to identify. They list terrorists, major criminals, and drug traffickers as key enemies, and point out that these people or groups may move from country to country and from location to location. Intelligence agencies are increasingly working with police forces and other law enforcers such as customs officers in order to gain information in the fight against 21st-century targets. But the introduction of thousands of closed circuit TV (CCTV) cameras in towns and cities and the use of computers to monitor phone and Internet traffic has caused much concern. Many people believe that the prospect of ordinary people being spied upon is a severe invasion of privacy.

Espionage has a long history and is considered a vital tool of government and military forces. Yet most of the time, the work is carried out in secret.

The need for intelligence

"Secret intelligence gives the Government a vital edge in tackling some of the most difficult problems we face ... intelligence forewarns us of threats to our national security; helps the Government promote international stability; provides support and protection to our forces; contributes to our economic health; and strengthens our efforts against terrorism and serious crime."

Tony Blair, prime minister of the UK

Democracy dies behind closed doors

Federal law enforcement agencies have assumed an unprecedented amount of authority to detain and spy on individuals. Yet the public has been kept unaware of how these powers have been used. Government secrecy is a concept completely at odds with the idea of government accountability. As U.S. District Court Judge Damon Keith said of the need to open up deportation hearings, "Democracy dies behind closed doors."

Source: American Civil Liberties Union

Governments maintain that this is necessary, but the vast majority of spies and operations that the public hears about are those in the distant past, or those that were uncovered or failed. Many pressure groups in the United States, the United Kingdom, and elsewhere have campaigned for less secrecy and greater openness in government and in the intelligence organizations. They argue that the public has a right to know what these agencies are doing on their country's behalf, and whether it is against the law or against the wishes of the majority of the people.

Espionage is a major industry. It costs billions of dollars to run and employs hundreds of thousands of people. Some critics wonder whether threats are exaggerated by intelligence organizations, who may even spread disinformation in order to maintain their importance and increase their budgets. But opponents point to the many major crimes, the rise in

Protecting the Olympics

At the 2000 Sydney Olympics, the Australian Security and Intelligence Organization (ASIO) performed more than 400 investigations into potential security threats to the Olympics. In the Athens 2004 games, a force of approximately 45,000 staff sought to enforce security.

the use and sale of illegal drugs, and major terrorist actions such as the destruction of the World Trade Center, as proof that the threats certainly exist. Intelligence is not always foolproof, as the failure to find large amounts of weapons of mass destruction in Iraq in 2003 and 2004 illustrates. This can mean that for some people, doubts remain as to whether an honest mistake was made or disinformation was practiced.

Detecting espionage and disinformation is incredibly difficult for ordinary people. Much of the work is shrouded in secrecy, and this can mean that various rumors and disinformation can flourish. Looking back through history and studying now-declassified secret files reveals some of the many ways in which espionage and disinformation can occur. Many of these methods remain in use today. For some, espionage is a threat to people's freedoms, is costly, and in many instances is morally wrong. To others, it is dirty but necessary work that must be done in order to protect ordinary people from extraordinary threats.

Alleged disinformation against France

The French Ambassador to the United States complained to the U.S. Congress in 2003 about alleged disinformation against France. France opposed the invasion of Iraq led by the United States and claimed that disinformation was published in the U.S. media to suggest that:

French officials issued French passports to Iraqi leaders wanted by the United States, allowing them to escape.

France supplied equipment to make nuclear weapons in 1998.

France possessed certain biological weapons prohibited by international agreements.

Source: BBC News

Committing espionage

Committing espionage against your own nation is a crime in all countries. In the United States, the most severe punishment allowed under the law for an act of espionage is death. In the United Kingdom, a spy from another country could face a prison term of up to 14 years. If the spy is a British citizen, the most severe punishment available is life in prison.

al-Qaeda
organization founded in the Middle East that is hostile to the United States and its allies

ASIO
Australian Security and Intelligence Organization, formed in 1949

assassin
secret service agent or person paid to plan and carry out the killing of a person considered a threat

boycott
refuse to have dealings with an organization, country, etc. in a protest of some kind

bugs
hidden devices, usually containing microphones and a transmitter, that can collect conversations and other sounds

CCTV
closed circuit television, a system of security cameras used in public places or inside and outside buildings

CIA
Central Intelligence Agency of the United States, founded in 1947

cipher
form of code in which each letter of the alphabet is represented by another letter, number, or symbol

code
letters, numbers, or symbols used to represent words and sentences in order to conceal the real meaning of a secret message

Cold War
hostile relationship between the Soviet Union and its allies and the United States and its allies that started shortly after World War II

counter-intelligence
information gathered and activities conducted to protect against espionage by others

coup or coup d'etat
forcible overthrow of a government by its opponents

courier
agent belonging to a spy network who retrieves and delivers messages, documents, film, or any other form of secret information

cover
false name, story, and background that disguises the real name, work, and purpose of a spy in enemy territory

cryptography
science of creating codes and ciphers

declassified
official information, such as political or military information, that is no longer secret and, in many countries, can be viewed by the public

defector
person who has left their own country's intelligence organizations to work for or pass information to another country

disinformation
information, known to be untrue by the sender, that is deliberately spread to deceive its audience

dissident
person who publicly disagrees with and criticizes their country or government and its policies

double agent
agent who has come under the control of another intelligence service and is being used against their original agency

espionage
spying, or the use of spies to obtain information

FBI
Federal Bureau of Investigation, the national police force and counter-espionage agency of the United States

industrial espionage
spying on companies or organizations to learn what new products, innovations, and plans they have

hate-mail
letter or some other form of correspondence that expresses anger, loathing, or prejudice, often using threats and offensive language

infiltrate
secretly enter a group or rival intelligence organization in order to spy on it

informer
someone who passes on important information to an intelligence organization or the police

intelligence
secret and potentially important and valuable information or news about an enemy or rival

KGB
acronym for State Security Committee, the former Soviet Union's key secret service, formed in 1954

MI5
British security service responsible for counter-espionage activities in the United Kingdom

MI6
British secret intelligence service responsible for foreign intelligence

mole
enemy agent who infiltrates a rival security service, sending intelligence back to a rival agency

Mossad
Israel's foreign intelligence agency, the Institute for Intelligence and Special Operations, formed in 1951

network
group of spies who may or may not know about each other, organized under the control of one spymaster

NRO
U.S. National Reconnaissance Office, responsible for surveillance and collecting intelligence from aerial reconnaissance and satellites

NSA
U.S. National Security Agency, responsible for collecting intelligence from communications such as radio signals, and for conducting cryptography

OSS
U.S. Office of Strategic Services, created in 1942 to perform spying and sabotage missions during World War II

PLO
Palestine Liberation Organization, a political body representing the Palestinian people, founded in 1964

sleeper
agent who lives as an ordinary citizen for many years before becoming operational

Soviet Union/USSR
established in 1917, dissolved in 1991, the Union of Soviet Socialist Republics (USSR) or Soviet Union, became the rival superpower to the United States after World War II

spymaster
agent in charge of a network or ring of spies. The term is also sometimes used for the head of an intelligence service

Stasi
East German State Security service that operated from 1950 to 1989

StB
Czech intelligence and security service

superpower
term used to describe the United States and the Soviet Union during the Cold War (1940s–1991)

surveillance
close observation of a place, person, or group over a period of time

SVR
Russia's foreign intelligence service, founded in 1991

taps
devices that allow the monitoring and recording of telephone calls

walk-in
someone who volunteers information or offers to work as a spy for an enemy intelligence agency

weapons of mass destruction
weapons, including chemical, biological, and nuclear weapons, that are designed to kill very large numbers of people

Books

Binns, Tristan Boyer. *The CIA*. Chicago: Heinemann Library, 2003.

Binns, Tristan Boyer. *The FBI*. Chicago: Heinemann Library, 2003.

Butler, William S. and L. Douglas Keeney. *Secret Messages*. New York: Simon & Schuster, 2001.

Gifford, Clive. *Spies*. Boston, Mass.: Kingfisher, 2004.

Hunter, Ryan Ann. *In Disguise: Real Stories of Women Spies*. Hillsboro, Ore.: Beyond Words, 2004.

Melton, H. Keith. *Ultimate Spy*. New York: DK Publishing, 2002.

Owen, David. *Hidden Secrets: A Complete History of Espionage and the Technology Used to Support It*. Richmond Hill, Ontario: Firefly, 2002.

Volkman, Ernest. *Espionage: The Greatest Spy Operations of the Twentieth Century*. New York, Wiley: 1996.

Organizations

Central Intelligence Agency
Office of Public Affairs
Washington, D.C. 20505

Dept. of Homeland Security
Office of Public Affairs
Washington, D.C. 20528

Federal Bureau of Investigation
J. Edgar Hoover Building
935 Pennsylvania Avenue, NW
Washington, D.C. 20535-0001

International Spy Museum
800 F Street, NW
Washington, D.C. 20004

National Security Agency
9800 Savage Road, Suite 6740
Fort Meade, MD 20755-6740